America Goes to War

The Civil War

by Kerry A. Graves

Consultant:
Stephen E. Osman
Historic Fort Snelling, Minnesota

CAPSTONE BOOKS
an imprint of Capstone Press
Mankato, Minnesota

Capstone Books are published by Capstone Press
151 Good Counsel Drive, P.O. Box 669, Mankato, Minnesota 56002
http://www.capstone-press.com

Library of Congress Cataloging-in-Publication Data

Graves, Kerry A.
    The Civil War/by Kerry A. Graves.
    p. cm.—(America goes to war)
    Includes bibliographical references and index.
    Summary: Describes the events leading up to the Civil War, the major conflicts,
the lives of the soldiers, and the outcome of the war.
    ISBN 0-7368-0582-6
    1. United States—History—Civil War, 1861-1865—Juvenile literature. [1. United
States—History—Civil War, 1861-1865.] I. Title. II. Series.

    E468.G766 2001
    973.7—dc21   00-025824

Editorial Credits
Blake Hoena, editor; Timothy Halldin, cover designer and illustrator; Katy Kudela,
    photo researcher

Photo Credits
Archive Photos, cover, 8, 24, 27, 28, 36, 38, 41
Corbis/Bettmann, 32
FPG International LLC, 6, 10, 12, 14, 17, 21, 30, 35
North Wind Picture Archives, 18

1 2 3 4 5 6 06 05 04 03 02 01

Table of Contents

Features

Fast Facts

Names and Dates: The Civil War sometimes is called the War Between the States, War of the Rebellion, or War of Northern Aggression. It began April 12, 1861, and officially ended April 9, 1865.

Start of the War: The Southern states left the United States and formed a separate country. They became the Confederate States of America. These Southern states included South Carolina, Mississippi, Florida, Alabama, Georgia, Louisiana, and Texas. Virginia, Arkansas, North Carolina, and Tennessee joined the Confederate States after the battle at Fort Sumter, South Carolina.

Issues of the War: Northern and Southern states disagreed about whether to have a strong central government or strong state governments. They also argued about whether to expand slavery into new territories.

Battle Locations: Battles occurred through the middle Atlantic and southeastern states. They ranged from Florida to Pennsylvania and west to the Mississippi and Ohio Rivers.

Major Battles: First Battle of Bull Run (July 1861); Battle of Antietam (September 1862); Battle of Gettysburg (July 1863); General William Sherman's "March to the Sea" (May to September 1864), from Atlanta to Savannah, Georgia

Armies: Armies in the Civil War were named according to the area where they operated.

Union: The U.S. Armies included the Army of the Potomac, the Army of the Ohio, and the Army of the Cumberland. Confederate soldiers nicknamed Union troops "Yankees."

Confederacy: The Confederate Armies included the Army of Northern Virginia, the Army of the Tennessee, and the Army of the West of the Confederacy. U.S. troops called Confederate soldiers "Rebels."

Important Leaders:

Union: President Abraham Lincoln, Major General George McClellan, Lieutenant General Ulysses S. Grant, Major General William Sherman, Major General Philip Sheridan

Confederacy: President Jefferson Davis, General Robert E. Lee, General Thomas "Stonewall" Jackson, General Joseph Johnston, Major General James Ewell Brown Stuart

Weapons Used: Soldiers mainly fought with muskets, rifles, and cannons. Soldiers first used machine guns, armored ships, and land and water mines during the Civil War.

End of the War: On April 9, 1865, Lee surrendered to Grant at Appomattox Courthouse in Virginia. Other Confederate Armies soon followed.

Chapter 1

Before the War

In 1861, people in the Southern and Northern regions of the United States lived very different lifestyles. The North's economy was based on industry and growing food crops. In the South, the economy depended on agriculture. Farmers grew export crops such as cotton and tobacco. Traders sold these crops to countries overseas.

Divided over Slavery

The different economies in the Northern and Southern states led to disagreements about slavery. Southern states favored slavery. Many Southern farmers used slaves to work on their plantations. Most Northern states opposed slavery. Southerners felt that this view threatened their way of life.

Abraham Lincoln was president of the United States during the Civil War.

The right to own slaves was an important issue between Northern and Southern states.

Slavery was illegal in many states in the northern, midwestern, and western United States. Most slave states were located in the southern and southeastern parts of the country. Texas, Missouri, Arkansas, Louisiana, Kentucky, Tennessee, and Mississippi were slave states. Other slave states included Alabama, Delaware, Maryland, Virginia, North Carolina, South Carolina, Georgia, and Florida.

States' Rights

Each state's position on slavery depended on whether it agreed with the North or the South on other issues. One disagreement between the North and South involved the power of individual states. Northern states believed in a strong central government. This government would have the power to make laws for all states. The South believed each state should have the power to make its own laws and govern itself. This issue was called states' rights.

Southerners feared that the North's larger population would pass national laws that would hurt the South's economy. These laws might have taxed crops that the South sold or they might have ended slavery. Some Southern leaders believed individual states should not have to follow federal laws with which they disagreed. These leaders felt that states should have more power than the federal government. This idea was unpopular in the North.

Issues of the War

Another disagreement between the North and the South involved territories in the western part of

the United States. These territories had not yet been divided into states. The U.S. Congress also had not decided if slavery would be legal in these areas when they became states.

Each new state would elect senators and representatives to serve in Congress. People believed that these new congress members' positions on slavery would affect their positions on other issues as well.

Economic differences caused other disagreements between the North and the South. Northern banks and businessmen usually owned the ships used to transport crops. They charged high fees to Southerners to move their goods overseas. Many Southerners thought that these prices were unfair.

Secession

Before the Civil War, only one in four Southern farmers owned slaves. But many slave owners in the South were rich and powerful. They helped make the laws in Southern states. They also helped decide U.S. laws.

Jefferson Davis was elected president of the Confederate States of America.

The Confederate attack on Fort Sumter began the Civil War.

Abraham Lincoln promised not to expand slavery into the new territories during the 1860 presidential election. This position angered many Southern politicians. When Lincoln won the election, South Carolina decided to secede from the United States. South Carolina no longer wanted to be governed by U.S. laws.

By February 1861, Mississippi, Alabama, Georgia, Florida, Louisiana, and Texas had joined South Carolina. They formed a new nation called the Confederate States of America.

Two Presidents

The Confederate leaders elected Jefferson Davis of Mississippi as their president. Davis had been a congressman, senator, and secretary of war in the U.S. government. In March 1861, he called for Southern men to volunteer for the Confederate Army. These soldiers took control of many U.S. forts and harbors in the South. They also stockpiled weapons. Richmond, Virginia, became the Confederate capital.

President Lincoln did not agree that states should be allowed to separate from the United States. He felt it was his duty to preserve the union of states. He announced that he would not begin a war with the Southern states. But he said it was wrong of the Confederacy to take control of U.S. forts in the South. One of these Southern forts was Fort Sumter in South Carolina. This fort was on an island in Charleston's harbor.

President Davis gave the command for his forces to take control of Fort Sumter. On April 12, Confederate soldiers fired cannons at Fort Sumter. The Union forces stationed there were outnumbered and soon surrendered. This battle began the Civil War.

Chapter 2

A Call to Arms

States began to choose sides with the Union or the Confederacy after Fort Sumter's surrender. Virginia, North Carolina, Tennessee, and Arkansas joined the Confederacy. But people who lived in the western part of Virginia did not favor the South's ideas. This region joined the Union and became what is now the state of West Virginia.

The states of Delaware, Maryland, Kentucky, and Missouri could not choose a side to support. They did not want to leave the Union. But slavery was legal in these states. They also supported some Southern issues. These states decided to remain neutral during the war.

Patriotism and the excitement of war convinced many volunteers to join the army.

To Be a Soldier

Patriotism led the first soldiers to join U.S. and Confederate Armies. These men felt a strong loyalty toward the ideas their governments supported.

Thousands of men joined the Union and Confederate armies by signing up at recruiting offices in their hometowns. Each state also had its own militia. These local military groups and the volunteers were then sent to Washington, D.C., or Richmond to train. New recruits believed soldiers led lives of excitement and adventure. The promise of a new uniform, weapons, and a short, exciting war convinced many young men to enter the army.

There were few requirements to be a soldier. The minimum age was 18. But many younger teenagers lied about their age in order to enlist. It is estimated that more than 800,000 Union soldiers were younger than 18. Women were not allowed to serve. Later in the war, some African Americans fought for the Union.

Uniforms

Soldiers wore many styles of uniforms at the beginning of the war. Each state militia had its own uniform. These colorful costumes sometimes were made by women in the soldiers' hometowns. Some state militias did not have enough money to provide

Volunteers were needed to fight in the U.S. Army.

new uniforms. These soldiers dressed in their everyday clothes. Soldiers who were already in the Union Army had official uniforms. They wore dark blue coats and trousers. Confederate soldiers had to invent a new uniform for their army.

The many styles of uniforms caused problems. Officers sometimes were not able to identify their own troops on the battlefield. Union officers mistook a group of Confederate soldiers dressed in blue for Union troops during the first Battle of Bull Run. This mistake allowed the Confederate soldiers to capture several Union cannons.

Many Southern officers had trained at the U.S. Military Academy in West Point, New York.

Both armies soon chose regular colors for uniforms to avoid further errors. The Confederate Army chose uniforms of gray coats and pants. The Union Army kept the official blue uniform that it had used before the war began.

Strengths and Weaknesses

The North seemed to have all the advantages at the beginning of the war. The Union's population was much larger than the Confederacy's. About 21 million people lived in Northern states. About 9 million people lived in the South. But a third of these people were African-American slaves.

The North also had a strong system of factories. These factories produced most of the manufactured goods in the United States. Factories also could be used to create military supplies such as weapons and uniforms. The South had to import many of its military supplies from foreign countries.

More than two-thirds of the country's railroads were located in Northern states. This allowed the North to easily transport supplies where needed.

The South had the advantage of stronger military training. Many Confederate officers had trained at the U.S. Military Academy in West Point, New York. They left the U.S. Army to fight for the Confederacy as soon as the war began. Also, many Southern men were familiar with hunting weapons and knew how to ride horses. These skills allowed the South to create skilled armies more quickly than the North. Many Northern soldiers had grown up in cities and were shopkeepers or factory workers. They had to learn the fighting skills that Southern soldiers already possessed.

Battle Plans

The two sides had very different battle plans. The North developed the "Anaconda Plan." They named this plan after a snake that squeezes its victims to death. It involved a naval blockade. Union ships would stop supplies from reaching Southern ports.

On land, Union forces would invade the South and separate it into sections. The Union planned to take control of the Mississippi River. This action would separate Texas, Missouri, Arkansas, and Louisiana from the rest of the Confederacy. These states then would be easier to defeat. The Union Army also planned to attack the Confederate capital of Richmond.

The Confederates needed to defend their territory and wear down Union forces. Most battles would be fought on their own land. This gave them an advantage. They knew the land and could easily travel over it. They also had easier access to their supplies.

President Davis hoped Great Britain and France would support the South. Crops such as cotton and tobacco were in demand in Europe. The South needed foreign trade to add to its limited supplies.

Types of Soldiers
Union and Confederate land armies included three types of military units. These units were cavalry, artillery, and infantry units.

Artillery units used cannons in battle.

Cavalry troops rode horses into battle. They could easily and rapidly move about the countryside. Their main job was to scout for enemy forces.

Artillery forces used cannons. Teams of horses pulled cannons to battle sites. Trains sometimes moved larger cannons. Many of these cannons were put into permanent locations at forts or on ships.

Infantry soldiers made up the largest part of Civil War armies. These foot soldiers usually marched to battle sites.

Gettysburg

Antietam

Bull Run (Manassas)

Washington, D.C.

Fredericksburg

Richmond

Appomattox Courthouse

Petersburg

Seven Days'
Battles

Monitor
and
Merrimac

Chickamauga

Fort Sumter

Atlanta

Sherman's
March to the Sea

Savannah

N

W   E

S

Confederacy

Union

Chapter 3

Early Battles

Both Union and Confederate leaders thought the war would end quickly. Union soldiers signed up to fight for only three months. By July 1861, most of these troops were near the end of their contracts. No battles had been fought. Union leaders felt they needed to attack the Confederacy even though their troops were not fully trained.

Union forces moved toward the Confederate Army at Manassas, Virginia. The soldiers were followed by hundreds of politicians, reporters, and sightseers. These onlookers believed the Union would defeat the Confederacy in only one battle.

But that did not happen. General Thomas "Stonewall" Jackson encouraged the Confederate

The Battle of Antietam was one of the bloodiest battles of the Civil War.

troops to victory. Their attack made the untrained Union troops panic and flee the battlefield. Confederate leaders became confident after this easy victory. Union leaders became overly cautious because of their defeat. These attitudes affected the early battles in the Civil War.

Eastern Battles

The Confederacy controlled the land battles in the East during the first two years of the war. It also controlled the Shenandoah Valley farmland in Virginia. This land provided the South with food supplies. The valley also was a pathway to the North through the Appalachian Mountains.

In late June, the Confederate Army protected Richmond from Union troops in the Seven Days' Battles. It also had a second victory at Bull Run in August. These victories convinced Confederate forces to try an offensive move. They marched through the Shenandoah Valley into Maryland. On September 17, 1862, they attacked Union forces in the Battle of Antietam. More than 23,000 soldiers died or were wounded during the battle. It was the war's bloodiest day of fighting. The Union won this battle.

Later battles took place near the Confederate capital. In December 1862, Union forces captured Fredericksburg, Virginia. But they were unable to capture Richmond. In May 1863, the Confederates defeated the Union Army at Chancellorsville, Virginia. But General Jackson died in the battle.

Western Battles

In the West, Union and Confederate forces battled for control of the Tennessee, Cumberland, and Mississippi Rivers. In February 1862, the Confederacy lost control of Fort Henry and Fort

Donelson in northwestern Tennessee. Brigadier General Ulysses S. Grant led the Union in these victories. Confederate forces had to retreat south without these forts to protect their supply shipments.

In April 1862, Grant stopped a Confederate attack at the Battle of Shiloh in Tennessee. The Union also forced the Confederates to retreat from Tennessee at the Battle of Stone's River near Murfreesboro.

Sea Battles

At first, the naval blockade was the only part of the Anaconda Plan that was successful. The Union built new steam-powered ships for the war. By 1861, the Union Navy included more than 260 ships.

Union victories in the summer of 1861 led to its control of several ports along the Atlantic coast. These ports included Port Royal and Hilton Head, South Carolina. In April 1862, the Union Navy captured New Orleans, Louisiana. This victory allowed Union ships to enter the Mississippi River from the Gulf of Mexico.

The Confederacy had few shipbuilding factories. They purchased ships from Great

Both the South and the North developed ironclad ships.

Britain. Confederate forces also captured some Union ships. The Confederate Navy rebuilt one of these ships. This ship was called the *Merrimac* and was renamed *Virginia* by the Confederates. The sides of this ship were covered with thick iron plates.

The Union hurried to build its own ironclad ship called the *Monitor*. On March 9, 1862, these two ships battled. Their iron plating protected them from harm. But several wooden ships were destroyed during the battle. These ships included the USS *Minnesota* and USS *Cumberland*.

Wounded soldiers often had to wait hours or days for treatment.

Care of Casualties

In 1861, the North and South had few well-trained doctors. Doctors' training usually involved two years of medical school with little hands-on practice.

Conditions in battlefield hospitals were especially bad. Medical supplies were scarce. Doctors often performed operations outdoors. Clean water often was not available. Doctors did not wash their hands or instruments between patients. This practice led to the spread of infections. These illnesses caused by germs killed many soldiers.

Field hospitals sometimes were as much as 1 mile (1.6 kilometers) away from battle sites. Many of the wounded soldiers had to walk to hospitals. They then had to wait hours or days for treatment. This long wait led to fevers and infections for many soldiers.

Injured soldiers often recovered in nearby houses or barns. Most of these buildings were crowded and dirty.

Disease was a problem even for soldiers who were not wounded. Many had never been exposed to illnesses such as chicken pox, measles, or mumps. These diseases killed many soldiers before they ever went to battle.

Dirty camps led to thousands of deaths from disease. Dysentery was the most common disease during the Civil War. In 1862, the Army of the Potomac reported 995 of every 1,000 soldiers suffered from this intestinal disease. Two soldiers died from disease for every soldier killed in battle during the Civil War.

Chapter 4

Life in Camp

A soldier's first experience in an army camp came when he reported for training. The strict schedule at camp included marching drills and bayonet practice. These metal blades attached to the end of soldiers' muskets. Soldiers also performed guard duty, dug ditches, cared for horses, and gathered food and water.

Soldiers carried only a few items as they marched to battle. They carried half of a two-man "pup" tent for shelter. They rolled their tent and extra clothes inside their blankets. Soldiers carried this bedroll over one shoulder as they marched.

Soldiers often had to march for days in a row. During long marches, they often did not want to

Army camps were soldiers' first experience with the army.

Soldiers often cooked and ate together.

take the time to unpack at night, set up camp, and repack their belongings the next morning. They then would sleep on the ground.

Armies did not battle during the winter because of the cold weather. Solders then would build more permanent camps. Four or more soldiers would build a log hut together. These shelters were warmer than cloth tents.

Soldiers had more free time during the winter months. Drills were canceled during bad weather. Men used this time to write letters, read, cook, and wash their clothes. Soldiers sang songs and played music, had snowball fights, and told stories to each other.

Supplies for the Troops
Civilian workers produced supplies for the troops in both the North and South. Soldiers left their jobs when they enlisted. These jobs were filled by people on the home front. Women and children often worked on farms and in factories.

Safe delivery of supplies was the duty of the Quartermaster Department. This army branch provided soldiers with food, clothing, weapons and ammunition, medical supplies, tents, wagons, and horses. It also rented ships, built docks, and maintained roads, rail lines, and bridges used to deliver supplies.

Meal Time
Soldiers in both armies struggled to find enough food. Supply wagons often could not keep up as troops marched between battle sites. Meat such as beef or pork was packed in salt water to

preserve it. Instead of fresh vegetables, Union soldiers received dried cakes made of pressed bits of potatoes, carrots, and other vegetables. Soldiers reported finding pieces of roots and leaves in the cakes and called them "baled hay."

Food rations differed between the Union and Confederacy. Rations also depended on available supply lines. As the war continued, Union soldiers received supplies more regularly than Confederate soldiers.

Soldiers often received hardtack instead of bread. These flour and water crackers were thick and so hard that soldiers called them "teeth dullers." Weevils often burrowed into the hardtack. Soldiers joked that these insect larvae were their only source of fresh meat.

When supplies were delayed, soldiers in both armies foraged the surrounding area for food. Hungry soldiers stole fruit from orchards and supplies from people's homes. They also raided barns and pastures for chickens, pigs, sheep, or cows. Men hunted wild game or picked wild berries as they marched.

Robert E. Lee (1807-1870)

Lee was born January 9, 1807, in Stratford, Virginia. In 1825, he entered the U.S. Military Academy at West Point, New York. Lee served as an engineer officer during the Mexican War (1846–1848). In 1852, he became superintendent of West Point. President Lincoln chose Lee to be commander of the Union Army. But he refused and joined the Confederate Army in 1861. President Davis appointed him commander of the Army of Virginia. In 1865, Lee was named General-in-Chief of the Armies of the Confederate States. That same year, he surrendered to Union General Ulysses S. Grant at Appomattox Courthouse. After the war, he was appointed president of Washington College in Lexington, Virginia. He died in Lexington, Virginia, in 1870.

Chapter 5

Final Battles

Many early battles of the Civil War were Confederate victories. But in 1863, that trend changed.

In May, Union General Ulysses S. Grant led two attacks against Vicksburg, Mississippi. This city was important for the control of travel on the Mississippi River. But Grant's forces were unable to capture Vicksburg. He then decided to lay siege to the city. This action prevented supplies from reaching Confederate troops there.

General Robert E. Lee decided to attack Union territory. He hoped this raid would draw troops away from Grant's siege. In late June, Lee arrived near Gettysburg, Pennsylvania. A small battle began when enemy patrol groups met. This fight then expanded into a three-day battle. The Union

General Ulysses S. Grant commanded the Union forces.

A small battle between Union and Confederate patrol groups led to the Battle of Gettysburg.

won the battle. More than 28,000 men in Lee's army were killed or wounded. The troops at Vicksburg then surrendered on July 4. These two losses lowered the spirits of Confederate troops.

Union control of the Mississippi River cut the Confederacy in half. Western food supplies then could no longer reach troops in the East.

Major General Sherman

Grant ordered Union Major General William Sherman to destroy the South's resources. Grant hoped this would help him defeat the South.

Sherman's troops moved from Atlanta to Savannah, Georgia, in a strip 60 miles (97 kilometers) wide. They did not rely on supply lines as they marched. Instead, they foraged for food along the way. Sherman's troops destroyed farms, railroads, warehouses, and factories. This robbed the Confederacy of needed supplies.

General Grant

Union losses in the first three years of the war resulted in changes in its army's leadership. On March 9, 1864, President Lincoln named Grant as general-in-chief of all Union armies.

Grant led a force of Union soldiers toward Richmond, Virginia. On May 5, Lee attacked these Union forces west of Chancellorsville, Virginia. Neither army was victorious.

Grant decided to bypass Lee's army and move closer to Richmond. Lee also moved his forces. They fought again at Spotsylvania. Grant then decided to try to take control of Petersburg. This town is located about 25 miles (40 kilometers) southeast of Richmond. He was unable to defeat Lee's forces and began a siege of the town.

Union victories and hardships in the South led to a great number of desertions from Lee's army. On April 2, his troops were unable to defeat Grant's forces. Lee's army then retreated. But the Union Army followed closely. On April 8, the Union Army surrounded Lee's forces at Appomattox Courthouse. Instead of starting another battle, Lee arranged to meet with Grant.

Lee's Surrender

Lee and Grant met on April 9, 1865. Grant had talked with President Lincoln during the siege of Petersburg. They already had discussed the terms of surrender for the Confederacy. Many people in the North felt that the Confederate leaders should be punished. But Lincoln felt they had suffered enough during the war. He wanted to reunite the two halves of the country as quickly and peacefully as possible.

Generous terms of surrender were the first step. Southern soldiers would give up their rifles. But they would be able to return to their homes immediately. Soldiers who owned a horse or mule would be allowed to take them home to work their farms. Hungry Confederate soldiers even received rations.

Word of the surrender spread quickly through the Union and Confederate forces at Appomattox

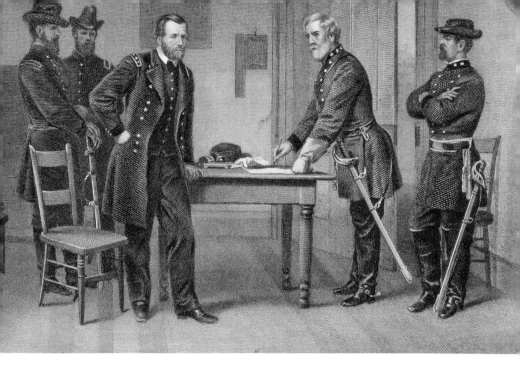

Lee surrendered to Grant on April 9, 1865, at Appomattox Courthouse.

Courthouse. The next day, Confederate soldiers turned in their weapons after a final speech from Lee. They then prepared to head home. Other groups of Confederate soldiers in Texas, North Carolina, Mississippi, and Alabama surrendered or were defeated by the Union Army by late May.

The war was finally over. The two halves of the United States were reunited. Congress also added the 13th amendment to the Constitution of the United States. This law made slavery illegal throughout the country.

Timeline

November—Abraham Lincoln is elected president of the United States.

December—South Carolina secedes.

March—Ironclad ships *Monitor* and *Merrimac* battle.

April—Battle of Shiloh takes place; the Union also captures New Orleans.

June—Seven Days' Battles begin.

August—Second Battle of Bull Run takes place.

1860

1862

1861

February—South forms Confederate States of America.

April—Confederate forces fire on Fort Sumter. This action begins the Civil War.

July—First Battle of Bull Run.

September—Battle of Antietam takes place.

December—Union captures Fredericksburg; Battle of Murfreesboro takes place.

January—Lincoln signs the Emancipation Proclamation. This act frees slaves in the South. Slavery then becomes the main issue of the war.

May—Union's first African-American unit is formed. Confederate General Jackson is killed in the Battle of Chancellorsville.

March—Lincoln places Grant in charge of the Union Army.

May—Battle of the Wilderness takes place.

November—Lincoln is reelected as president. Union Major General Sherman begins the "March to the Sea."

1863　　1864

1865

July—Battle of Gettysburg takes place. Union also captures Vicksburg and Port Hudson.

September—Battle of Chickamauga takes place.

November—Lincoln delivers Gettysburg Address.

April—Union forces capture Richmond. Lee surrenders. Lincoln is shot by John Wilkes Booth after the war is over.

December—Congress approves the 13th Amendment and makes slavery illegal in the United States.

Words to Know

artillery (ar-TIL-uh-ree)—a unit of soldiers who use cannons in battle

blockade (blok-ADE)—closing off an area to keep people or supplies from passing through

cavalry (CAV-uhl-ree)—a unit of soldiers who fight on horseback

infantry (IN-fuhn-tree)—a unit of soldiers who fight on foot

militia (muh-LISH-uh)—a group of civilians who serve as soldiers in emergencies; states during the Civil War had their own militias.

ration (RASH-uhn)—daily amount of food given to a soldier

secede (si-SEED)—to formally withdraw from a group or organization

siege (SEEJ)—the surrounding of a place to cut off supplies and wait for the trapped group to surrender

To Learn More

Blashfield, Jean F. *Mines and Minié Balls: Weapons of the Civil War.* A First Book. New York: Franklin Watts, 1997.

Dosier, Susan. *Civil War Cooking: The Union.* Exploring History through Simple Recipes. Mankato, Minn.: Blue Earth Books, 2000.

Ransom, Candice F. *Children of the Civil War.* Picture the American Past. Minneapolis: Carolrhoda Books, 1998.

Sandler, Martin W. *Civil War.* New York: HarperCollins Publishers, 1996.

Steele, Christy and Anne Todd, eds. *A Confederate Girl: The Diary of Carrie Berry, 1864.* Diaries, Letters, and Memoirs. Mankato, Minn.: Blue Earth Books, 2000.

Useful Addresses

Appomattox Courthouse National Historical Park
P.O. Box 218
Appomattox, VA 24522

Fort Sumter National Monument
1214 Middle Street
Sullivan's Island, SC 29482

Gettysburg National Military Park
97 Taneytown Road
Gettysburg, PA 17325

Museum of the Confederacy
1201 East Clay Street
Richmond, VA 23219

Internet Sites

The American Civil War
http://www.americancivilwar.com

American Memory–Library of Congress
    Selected Civil War Photographs
http://memory.loc.gov/ammem/cwphome.html

The Civil War Artillery Page
http://www.cwartillery.org/artillery.html

The History Place
http://www.historyplace.com

Turning Point: The American Civil War
http://prometheus.cc.emory.edu/TurningPoint
    /pages/index.htm

U.S. Military Academy Map Library–Civil War
http://www.dean.usma.edu/history/dhistorymaps/
    AcivilwarPages/ACWToC.htm

Index